The Mesilla Valley
AN OASIS IN THE DESERT

THE MESILLA VALLEY

AN OASIS IN THE DESERT

A NEW MEXICO CENTENNIAL HISTORY SERIES BOOK

Jon Hunner

with

Peter Dean, Frankie Miller, Jeffrey Schnitzer,
Christopher Schurtz, and Stephen Vann

SUNSTONE
PRESS

SANTA FE

Front Cover: Chiles packed into the "Fancy Chili Pepper" sacks signal the end
of the summer and will provide spice for foods through the winter.
(Courtesy of NMSULASP)

Sunstone books may be purchased for educational, business,
or sales promotional use. For information please write:
Special Markets Department, Sunstone Press,
P.O. Box 2321, Santa Fe, New Mexico 87504-2321.

Library of Congress Cataloging-in-Publication Data

Hunner, Jon.
 The Mesilla Valley : an oasis in the desert / by Jon Hunner ; with Peter Dean ...
[et al.].
    p. cm. -- (A New Mexico centennial history series book)
 Includes bibliographical references.
 ISBN 978-0-86534-627-7 (softcover : alk. paper)
 1. Mesilla Valley (N.M.)--History--Pictorial works. 2. Mesilla Valley (N.M.)--Pic-
torial works. I. Dean, Peter. II. Title.
 F802.M4H86 2008
 978.9'66040222--dc22

                              2008011554

WWW.SUNSTONEPRESS.COM
SUNSTONE PRESS / POST OFFICE BOX 2321 / SANTA FE, NM 87504-2321 /USA
(505) 988-4418 / ORDERS ONLY (800) 243-5644 / FAX (505) 988-1025

*F*or Mary Daniels Taylor, historian, photographer,
heritage preservationist, Mesillera.

Contents

Acknowledgements

Creating *The Mesilla Valley: An Oasis in the Desert* has involved many people working since 2005. Numerous students in the Public History Program at New Mexico State University have researched, written, and assembled this book, including Samantha Alaniz, Regina Burgess, Marty Davenport, Shannon Gray-Anderson, Terrence Faulkner, Jonathan Jefferson, Marvin Steinback, Katherine Swank, and Jeanne Wilkins. The final version of this book was compiled by Peter Dean, Frankie Miller, Jeffrey Schnitzer, Christopher Schurtz, Stephen Vann, and me. At the beginning of each chapter, those who worked on that chapter are acknowledged. The Rio Grande Historical Collection at the NMSU Library provided most of the photographs used in this book. The staff there—Dennis Daily, Chris Laumbach (who copied most of the photographs to a digital format), Lenny Silverman, and the RGHC director, Steven Hussman, deserve our many thanks. At the Institute for Historical Research, Director Evan Davies also allowed us to use some of their photographs for this book. Dr. Jeffrey Brown (the head of the Department of History at NMSU), Nancy Shockley (the department's administrator), Dr. Dulcinea Lara (our newest professor in the department), John McGuinn of the Campus Architects Office, Dr. Abran Lujan Aremendariz (of the NMSU College of Education), and Provost Waded Cruzado-Salas (while she was Dean of the College of Arts and Sciences) have supported this project. Senator Mary Jane Garcia, Representative J. Paul Taylor, and Pat Taylor consulted with us on the photos and captions in *The Mesilla Valley*. As the first in a series of books published by Sunstone Press to commemorate the centennial of New Mexico's statehood, we would also like to thank James Clois Smith, Jr. and Carl Condit for their support at Sunstone Press. *The Mesilla Valley* is a companion book to *Las Cruces: City of Crosses* that the Public History Program published in 2004. Since Las Cruces focused on the City of the Crosses, this book turns its attention elsewhere and covers the rest of this fascinating valley.

—Jon Hunner, Director, Public History Program
New Mexico State University, August 2007

A Brief History of an Oasis in the Desert

Near the border of the United States and Mexico exists a place considered by many as one of New Mexico's best-kept secrets, a fertile river valley where the Rio Grande bends and cuts into a long sloping mesa before heading south to El Paso and Mexico. The Mesilla Valley is thirty miles long and thirty miles wide, running from the Leasburg-Ft. Selden area in the north to the small town of Anthony, N.M. in the south and from the humble Robledo and Doña Ana mountains on the northwest to the spectacularly jagged peaks of the Organ Mountains that stretch like a spine along the valley's eastern rim.

Sprinkled along the river's banks and throughout the valley floor exist two dozen communities, from sparsely-populated rural hamlets and colonias to the second largest city in the state, Las Cruces (2007 pop. 90,000), the urban heart of the Mesilla Valley. No other feature has defined the Mesilla Valley more than the river that runs through it, the Rio Grande, a once free-running body of water prone to widespread, unpredictable flooding and changes in course. For almost a century, the Elephant Butte, Caballo, Leasburg, and Mesilla dams have regulated the natural flows and rhythms of the Rio Grande, enabling dependable irrigation and agriculture, as well as commercial and residential development of the valley.

The vast majority of human settlement of the valley is fairly recent, occurring over the past 150 years; however, archeological evidence indicates that for thousands of years small bands of American Indians, mostly Mogollon, their descendents the Mansos and the Tiwas, and later the Apaches, lived in the valley growing crops while subsisting on the hearty flora and fauna surrounding the Rio Grande. For various reasons, settlement of the Mesilla Valley in large numbers did not begin until the later half of the 19th century. While established as part of Mexico's most northern territory since the late 16th century, the Mesilla Valley largely escaped Spanish settlement and colonization. In short, the Mesilla Valley was merely another stopover, or paraje, along the Camino Real de Tierra Adentro (The Royal Road to the Interior Lands). This trade route extended from Mexico City to Santa Fe from 1598 to 1881.

Spanish conquistador Don Juan De Oñate, for whom a Las Cruces high school is named, was one of the first documented European explorers to see the Mesilla Valley, when his party passed through in 1598. The Robledo Mountains, the rolling range that shoulders the valley at its north end, are named for one of Oñate's party who died near the site. Only after the independence of Mexico in 1821 did the newly established Mexican government approve the first major land grants in the valley, and opened the Camino Real for the first time to Anglo traders.

This led in 1842 to the valley's first major settlement of Doña Ana (2007 pop. 1,400), the oldest continuously inhabited community along the Rio Grande in southern New Mexico. The Village of Doña Ana recently finished renovation of its historic Our Lady of Purification Catholic Church, an adobe structure noted as the oldest church in southern New Mexico. The town served as a foothold in the valley for future settlement, which increased when New Mexico was acquired by the United States in 1848 after the war with Mexico, and the Treaty of Guadalupe Hidalgo ceded all the land from Texas and California to the United States.

Las Cruces, founded on the site where crosses were erected for slain travelers, was plotted in 1849. It became the county seat of Doña Ana County, a pivotal railroad stop in 1881 and ultimately the Mesilla Valley's largest city. Nestled under the towering Organ Mountains, Las Cruces is also the geographic center of the valley, and one of its most picturesque and commanding locations.

The village of Mesilla (2007 pop. 2,200), which once sat on the west side of the Rio Grande in what was then Mexico, was founded in 1849 by several groups of Mexicans who did not wish to be part of the United States after the Mexican War. A regular stop on the Butterfield Overland Trail, Mesilla became part of the United States when an American flag was raised over its plaza in 1854 upon the ratification of the Gadsden Purchase. In the first years of the Civil War, the village was the capital of the Confederate Territory of Arizona.

Other valley communities, like La Mesa, La Union, Chamberino, Leasburg, and Picacho began popping up at the same time as Mesilla and Las Cruces. Promises of mineral wealth in the Organ Mountains drew thousands to the Mesilla Valley, and by the 1870s the scrappy town of Organ was one of the valley's fastest growing areas; however, soon after the turn of the century, the mines and the town were in decline. Several post-Civil War-era army forts, including Ft. Selden at the base of the Jornada del Muerto near Leasburg Dam, were built to secure the area from Indian attacks and bandit raids. Now a New Mexico State Monument, the fort's crumbling adobe walls still evoke the Wild West past.

Efforts to control the Rio Grande, which repeatedly flooded the valley's communities, began in the late 19th century, culminating in 1916 with the completion of the Elephant Butte Dam. Although the dam lies to the north, it forever affected the future of the Mesilla Valley, opening hundreds of thousands of acres to agricultural and urban development, as well as providing water in times of drought from one of the largest man-made reservoirs in the country.

An oasis in the desert, the Mesilla Valley contains much of the geographic diversity that defines the rest of New Mexico: rolling desert hills dotted with mesquite, yuccas, and creosote; lush valley floors teeming with acequia-fed fields and orchards, rocky mountain peaks stretching 9,000 feet into the air, a myriad of domestic and wild animals, as well as more pecan trees per square mile than almost anywhere else on earth.

The Mesilla Valley also contains human stories that are, as area historian Mary Taylor said of her beloved Mesilla in her book, "As Wild as the West Ever Was." Its history is of intrepid pioneers and blindly ambitious capitalists, of famous lawmen and infamous outlaws, of Civil War battles and struggles for statehood, of railroads and mining towns, of first generation immigrants searching for prosperity in various trades and businesses or for security in orchards, vineyards, and fields. Every story of the Old West is represented in the Mesilla Valley.

So too are stories of modernization, education, and economic progress. By the turn of the 20th century, the New Mexico College of Agricultural and Mechanic Arts, now New Mexico State University, was located three miles south of Las Cruces, earning the valley a reputation for agricultural and engineering studies. Home to the first radio station in New Mexico, the university is one of the oldest and most successful land grant colleges in the country, and serves more than 16,000 students from around the world.

At the turn of the 21st century more than 175,000 people of various cultures call the Mesilla Valley home. With a rich history to tell, the photographs in this book offer a glimpse, albeit a satisfying and fascinating one, into the interaction of multiple cultures, from Spanish and Mexican to Anglo and American Indian, and into the people and places that have defined the Mesilla Valley.

—Christopher Schurtz, Department of History
New Mexico State University, August 2007

1

Mesilla

Frankie Miller, Marvin Steinback,
Katie Swank, and Jeanne Wilkins

Dedication of San Albino. The dedication ceremony for the newly reconfigured San Albino Church in Mesilla was held in 1908. The church was named for Saint Albino, a bishop who helped the homeless, the poor, orphaned children, and widows. Parish priest Father Grange presided over the dedication. He lived in the Barela/Reynolds/Taylor House across the plaza of Mesilla, which is now a State Monument. (Courtesy of NMSULASP)

Commemoration of the Gadsden Purchase. The Treaty of Mesilla (also known as the Gadsden Purchase) was signed in Mexico City in December 1853. This famous painting by Albert Fountain Jr. depicts the flag raising ceremony on the plaza when General Garland, the representative of the United States presented the Mexican flag to General Angel Trias,

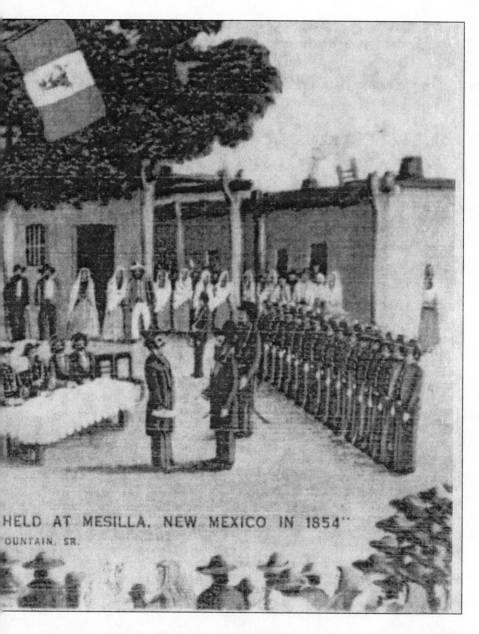

HELD AT MESILLA, NEW MEXICO IN 1854"
OUNTAIN, SR.

the governor of the state of Chihuahua. With that transfer, Mesilla was transferred from Mexico to the United States. The Gadsden Purchase completed the last addition of land to the continental United States. (Courtesy of NMSULASP)

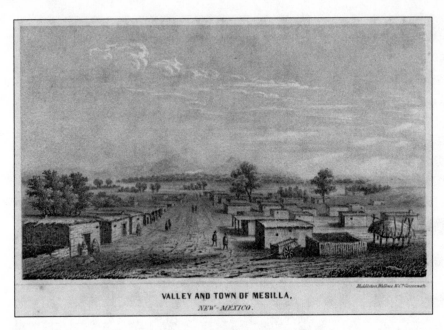

VALLEY AND TOWN OF MESILLA,
NEW-MEXICO.

The Village of Mesilla. The secession of Texas from Mexico in 1836 eventually resulted in the Mexican-American War (1846 to 1848). The victory of the United States sealed by the Treaty of Guadalupe Hidalgo transferred the Mexican territories of Alta California and Nuevo Mexico to the United States; however, Mexicans who did not want to live in the United States migrated to the west bank of the Rio Grande and created Mesilla in what was then still part of Mexico. The river flooded in the 1860s, and eventually settled on its present course west of Mesilla. (Courtesy of NMSULASP)

Mesilla Postcard. Although the year is smudged away, this postcard depicts the dusty streets of Mesilla on the first of May in the late 1800s. (Courtesy of NMSULASP)

Muddy Roads. Pools of water from heavy rains caused problems for animal drawn wagons and buggies. Torrential downpours during the summer monsoons fall too quickly for the soil to absorb the rain. Note the farmer in the distance who wore a sombrero to shade him from the intense summer sun. (Courtesy of NMSULASP)

Crumbling adobes. From 1849 to 1881, Mesilla was the biggest town in southern New Mexico. After the railroad went through Las Cruces instead of Mesilla in 1881, Mesilla lost its standing as the county seat within six months and was quickly eclipsed by the City of Crosses. By 1931, one observer remarked, "Since that time, Mesilla has largely been deserted and its old adobe houses have crumbled rapidly." (Courtesy of NMSULASP)

Dimetrio Chavez Store. Perhaps it is the owner himself who stands in front of the Dimetrio Chavez Store and Post Office in Mesilla at the southwest corner of the Plaza. After working for Joseph Reynolds, the previous owner for many years, Demetrio finally purchased the shop from him. (Courtesy of NMSULASP)

Casad Home. Thomas Casad came to Mesilla in 1874 and operated a flour mill while also farming grapes and fruit. When these crops failed, he switched his efforts to alfalfa and angora goats. Additionally, Casad purchased over 10,000 acres from the Brazito Land Grant in the southern part of the valley. (Courtesy of NMSULASP)

William E. Martin and Louise Newcomb Martin. Sunday drives did not begin with the automobile, but rather in a horse drawn buggy. The Victorian middle class enjoyed such leisurely drives through the countryside. (Courtesy of NMSULASP)

Horses, Burros, and Family. The Frenger family from left to right were Mrs. George Frenger, Raymond Frenger, and George Frenger. (Courtesy of NMSULASP)

Guadalupe Street around 1900. Looking north along Guadalupe Street, the Mesilla Plaza is on the left and what is now La Posta is on the right. The steeple of San Albino Church is just visible over the trees on the plaza in the distance. (Courtesy of NMSULASP)

Mesilla Procession. Altar boys and the Daughters of Mary (who are carrying the white flags) precede the saint in the procession of the Feast of San Albino. Father Kirgan took part in this celebration in the early 1950s. Visible behind the procession is the back of La Posta. (Courtesy of J. Paul and Mary Taylor)

San Albino Church (1890s). Here the former San Albino Church illustrates a different architectural style than the current church. (See 1st photo in this chapter). From this distinctive bell tower, the chimes were alarm clocks, alerted the community residents of the birth of a child or a death in the community, or even warned of danger. (Courtesy of NMSULASP)

Fountain Theater. Built in 1902, the Fountain Theater of Mesilla used to be called the Fountain of Pleasure Theater and the Fountain of Youth Theater. Until the 1920s, the theater featured live singing and dancing. In April 1861 during the Civil War, this site was rented to the Confederacy for their governmental headquarters. Today, efforts are underway to preserve and restore this important historic building. (Courtesy of NMSULASP)

Fountain Family Troubadours. Descendants of the prominent Mesilla resident Albert J. Fountain entertained themselves during the 1930s. The building in the background is the Griggs House which still stands. Col. Albert Fountain and his eight year old son Henry were mysteriously murdered in 1896, possibly by ranchers angered by his indictment of them on rustling charges. (Courtesy of NMSULASP)

Santiago Brito. Santiago was father of José, Frank, and Estefana Estanislada. (Courtesy of J. Paul and Mary Taylor)

Law Men. Santa Rosa Rico served as City Marshall of Las Cruces in 1920, and to his Left, Frank Brito was the constable of Precinct 29. Rico was the only survivor of an Indian Massacre on a wagon train belonging to Don Barbaro Lucero. Frank Brito was a member of the Rough Riders when he ran a stockade in Cuba where he was able to talk to the Spanish speaking prisoners during the Spanish-American War. He also served in Columbus, N.M. following Pancho Villa's raid in 1916. (Courtesy of NMSULASP)

The Barela/Reynolds/Taylor State Monument. Some of the oldest buildings on the plaza comprise the Barela/Reynolds/Taylor House, now part of New Mexico State Monuments. The Barela family started a store here in 1860, later operated by Joseph and William Reynolds. Mary and J. Paul Taylor bought it in 1953 and after living in it for a half a century, donated their home and storefronts to the state in 2004. (Photo by Jon Hunner)

Frank L. Oliver Store and Saloon. Near today's Don Felix Café in Mesilla, the Oliver store offered bridles, hitching equipment, barrels of whiskey, lager beer signs, chairs, and saddles. This is a perfect example of the multi-purpose business at the turn of the 20th century in southern New Mexico. (Courtesy of NMSULASP)

Otto Bombach General Store. Several persons including a customer, a store clerk, and the owner's son, John Bombach (who is standing at the counter) illustrate Mesilla mercantilism around 1907. The Otto Bombach store featured household goods including foodstuffs, shoes, clothing, and other general merchandise. (Courtesy of NMSULASP)

Hanging Out on the Corner. The Territorial architectural style of the 19th century remained the same into the 1930s in Mesilla. Notice the long, low windows coming nearly to street level and the ornate brick parapets along the tops of the building. (Courtesy of NMSULASP)

Fisticuffs in the Shade. Just ask any teacher — give children a few minutes of spare time and someone will start a fight. Two school-aged boys settle their dispute under the shade trees around 1900. (Courtesy of NMSULASP)

The Billy the Kid Bar. This building at the southeast corner of the plaza functioned as a store until after the Civil War, when the county obtained ownership and converted it into a courthouse, jail, and school. In April 1881, William Bonney, alias "Billy the Kid," was tried there and convicted for the murder of Sheriff William Brady. (Courtesy of NMSULASP)

Elephant Butte Saloon. In this building (the same as in the photo above), Hispanic businessman Florencio Lopez ran the Elephant Butte Saloon and billiard parlor from 1905 to 1913.In the picture from left to right are Juan Lopez, Frank Lopez, Gustavo Audetat, and Blas Pino. On May 10, 1911, A. J. (Joe) Lopez sold the Elephant Butte Saloon to his son Florencio Lopez for 300 pesos. (Courtesy of NMSULASP)

E.V. Gamboa Store. On the northeast corner of the plaza, the E. V. Gamboa store was one of many businesses on that block owned by the Gamboa family. In the early 20th century, the family lived in the second story over the store. (Courtesy of NMSULASP)

Thomas J. Bull Band on Calle Principal. Festivities in Mesilla included a mix of Anglo and Mexican culture. The Thomas J. Bull Band probably featured a combination of music to satisfy the varied cultural tastes of the area. (Courtesy of NMSULASP)

Mesilla Valley Entertainment. Before movies, radio, television, and iPods, bands such as these entertained the people of the Mesilla Valley and helped celebrate the rich mix of cultures with holidays such as Las Posadas at Christmas, Cinco de Mayo, and the Feast Day for St. Albino. (Courtesy of NMSULASP)

Main Street, Mesilla Park. Looking south on Main Street as it passes through Mesilla Park during the 1930s, the businesses and automobiles shared the town's dirt streets. Main Street used to be the main road to El Paso, Texas. Identifiable buildings that are still standing are the Texaco service station on the left and the Mesilla Park train depot on the right. (Courtesy of NMSULASP)

Atchison, Topeka & Santa Fe Railway, Station, Las Cruces New Mexico March 25, 1901

The Train Arrives. In 1881, the Atchison, Topeka, and Santa Fe Railroad transformed the Mesilla Valley. This photo in 1901 shows the train arriving at the depot in Las Cruces. (Courtesy of NMSULASP)

2

The Organ Mountains and the North Valley

Marty Davenport, Christopher Schurtz, and Stephen Vann

The Mesilla Valley. The old U.S. 70/80 highway descends from the west into the Mesilla Valley in 1947. In addition to providing a link to Arizona and the West Coast, U.S. 70 also served as an escape route from the Dust Bowl for many people during the Great Depression. (Courtesy of NMSULASP)

The Organ Mountains. A panoramic view shows major topographical features including Organ Peak (9002 feet), and Fillmore Canyon, which possessed the only permanent stream in the Organs. Little grass is visible in the photo but desert shrub species including yucca,

greasewood, and mesquite are evident. The main portions of the Organ Mountains consist of volcanic batholiths pushed up from the earth some 36,000,000 years ago (Courtesy of NMSULASP).

Van Patten's Camp. Built in the 1870s by Eugene Van Patten, this camp was later renamed Dripping Springs Resort. In 1907, it was sold to Dr. Nathan Boyd and converted into a sanatorium for treating tuberculosis patients. After years of disuse, it was purchased by The Nature Conservatory and handed over to the Bureau of Land Management for preservation and public recreational use. (Courtesy of NMSULASP)

Social Gathering. Eugene Van Patten, Alice Capps, Dr. Noah Bates, Ralph S. Paddock, and others gather at the Dripping Springs Resort. The resort's cool climate and beautiful views attracted many visitors, including Sheriff Pat Garret and General Pancho Villa. (Courtesy of NMSULASP)

Colonel Van Patten. Eugene Van Patten wore many hats in his day. He was, at varying times, a Confederate soldier, deputy U.S. marshal, militiaman, sheriff, and resort operator. In addition, he was instrumental in fighting for the rights of the Tortugas Indians. (Courtesy of NMSULASP)

Placer Mining. John Dodd and L.B. Bentley engage in placer mining in the Organ Mountains. Placer miners separate gold from dirt by hand with running water, as opposed to lode mining where ore is dug from tunnels deep out of the earth. Reports of gold derived from placer mining in the Organs date back to 1881. (Courtesy of NMSULASP)

Modoc Mine. The Modoc Mine operated from 1879 until 1905. Speculators invested heavily in the infrastructure of the Modoc Mine but overestimated the amount of valuable ore in the ground. Unfortunately for these investors, the yields failed to match the expectations. The mine, located near Dripping Springs, produced significant quantities of lead, but dreams of a silver or gold bonanza never materialized. (Courtesy of NMSULASP)

Modoc Machinery. A dry concentrator was used to reduce the size of rock-bearing ore before transportation. The Modoc Mine was described by W.G. Ritch as rich in silver, copper, and "a little gold." Unfortunately for William Ryerson, the mine's primary backer and a prominent lawyer and politician in Las Cruces, Ritch seems to have exaggerated the amount of precious ore available in the Modoc. (Courtesy of NMSULASP)

Mining Hoist. Several miners gather around a hand-cranked mining hoist. The machine was normally operated by two people, and used to transport heavy loads—including men—up and down into the mines below. (Courtesy of NMSULASP)

Interior of the Stephenson-Bennett Mine. Two miners use candlelight to illuminate the interior shoring of the mine. Before Hugh Stephenson bought the mine, workers carried heavy sacks of ore out of the mine on their backs while carefully climbing up pegs drilled into the walls of the shaft. (Courtesy of NMSULASP)

Mining in the Organs. A group of unidentified miners takes a break from work on a mine in the Organ Mountains. The prospect of mineral riches drew people from around the country to the Organs, and by the turn of the century, mining was a vibrant, if short lived, industry in the Mesilla Valley. (Courtesy of NMSULASP)

Women in the Mining Camps. The role of women in mining camps can be hard to determine. In addition to being spouses, camp women offered a variety of services to miners, including cooking, cleaning, sewing, entertainment, and prostitution. The small building in the back of this photo is typical of a "crib" in a mining camp. (Courtesy of NMSULASP)

Main Street, Organ, New Mexico. This scene in front of the Bentley Store, circa 1910, shows two sturdy wagons that carried the raw ore to the railroad stop in Las Cruces which took the ore to a smelter in El Paso. The stone and adobe building on the left is the Bentley Store and Assay Office where livery services, miners' tools, and general supplies were purchased. The building exists today and is on the New Mexico Register of Cultural Properties. (Courtesy of NMSULASP)

Footrace. Adults avoided the sun while children participated in a footrace in Organ on the Fourth of July around 1909. The extreme heat of the southwest made parasols more than a mere fashion statement, and men and women alike wore broad-brimmed hats to stave off the sun. (Courtesy of NMSULASP)

Organ Mining Camp. George Courtney guides his horse up to the Bentley building in Organ Camp. Horses remained an important mode of transportation well into the twentieth century in New Mexico, particularly in rural areas such as Organ and the Mesilla Valley. (Courtesy of NMSULASP)

Woman with Pet Crow. In the 1910s, young Charles Bentley found a baby crow and named it Jim Crow. At the time, Jim Crow also referred to the racial segregation in the country. According to local historian Herman Weisner, the crow flew from one saloon to another in Organ stealing coins right off the bar. Jim was blamed for pestering school children, pickpocketing drunks, and knocking laundry off the lines. One day after scaring children and spooking a horse, Jim flew into Logan's Bar where M. C. Logan shot and killed him. In the 1960s, Jim Crow's hiding place revealed some pilfered coins, one of which sold for $25. (Courtesy of NMSULASP)

L. B. Bentley, circa 1915. L.B. Bentley arrived in Organ around 1900 and lived there for the next fifty-five years. Besides running the general store, Bentley ran an ore assay business, was the postmaster, constable, miner, school board member, and ran a bar for several years. Although the mining boom ended when inflated copper prices plummeted after World War I, Bentley continued to offer assay services into the 1940s. (Courtesy of NMSULASP)

Boys with Dead Bobcat. Charles Bentley (son of L.B. Bentley), on the right, and an unknown boy display the bobcat they shot. Bobcats were considered nuisances and predators in 1915. A sizeable bounty on predators and sale of the pelts encouraged boys such as these to hunt and trap bobcats, cougars, and badgers. (Courtesy of NMSULASP)

Organ Schoolhouse. By 1907, copper production in the Organ Mining District reached an all time high and boosted the population to several hundred residents. A community effort to build a school resulted in this stone building, which still stands. Elizabeth Garrett, the blind daughter of famed lawman Pat Garrett and later authoress of the New Mexico state song, "O, Fair New Mexico," sang at fundraisers for the school. (Courtesy of NMSULASP)

Students at Organ. The pupils of Organ School pose outside the building in the early 1910s. A single teacher was responsible for the education of all the children, and perhaps because of the demands, many different people held the position during the school's existence. (Courtesy of NMSULASP)

Baylor Pass. A woman with rifle poses atop a mule near Baylor Pass in the Organ Mountains. Named after the Confederate Lieutenant Colonel John Baylor who declared southern New Mexico part of the "Confederate Territory of Arizona" during the Civil War, the pass continues to be a popular hiking and horseback riding destination. (Courtesy of NMSULASP)

Picnic in the Organs. Several locals enjoy a picnic in the Organ Mountains sometime around 1910, possibly near Dripping Springs Resort. The Organs have long served as a retreat for Mesilla Valley residents seeking cool relief from the heat. (Courtesy of NMSULASP)

The first Residence Building at SHALAM, six miles northwesterly from Las Cruces, New Mexico, 1889. (Shalam was a co-operative colony, established by Dr. John B. Newbrough and Andrew M. Howland, under the direction of the Inner Council of the TAE,-Faithists).

Searching For Utopia. Dr. John Newbrough and his followers established the Shalam Colony in 1884 west of Doña Ana on the banks of the Rio Grande. The colony brought orphans from around the country to be raised in the utopian community. Newbrough, a mystic who wrote his own bible, died of the flu in 1891, and although his followers tried to keep the colony going, it was eventually abandoned in 1901. (Courtesy of NMSULASP)

Fort Selden. First commissioned in 1865, Fort Selden served as a home to Army infantry and cavalry units, including the famed African-American "Buffalo Soldiers." The fort's primary purpose was to fight bandits and Apaches and patrol the Chihuahua Trail. (Courtesy of IHSF)

The Ruins of Fort Selden. The adobe walls of Fort Selden had already begun to melt back into the desert by the early 20th century when this picture was taken. Abandoned in 1895 and now a New Mexico State Monument, the old fort was a key installation in the settling of the West. (Courtesy of NMSULASP)

Radium Springs Inn. The Hot Springs Hotel and Bathhouse was constructed in 1931 at the site of natural hot springs along the banks of the Rio Grande. The property has been restored as a hotel and is listed on the New Mexico State Register of Cultural Properties. (Courtesy of NMSULASP)

Elephant Butte Dam. The Elephant Butte Dam (although north of the Mesilla Valley) changed the valley forever. After its completion in 1916, the 306 foot high dam created the world's largest man-made reservoir at the time. The dam regularized the flow of the river, reduced flooding, lessened drought conditions, opened up thousands of acres of land to farming, and provided hundreds of thousands of acre-feet of water a year. The dam took five years and more than $7,000,000 to complete. (Courtesy of NMSULASP)

"*El Hermitano*," the Hermit of La Cueva: Born in 1800, Giovanni Maria Agostini spent many years walking through Europe, North and South America, Mexico, and Cuba. He lived for a time on a mountain peak near Las Vegas, New Mexico before walking to Mesilla at age 67. For the next two years, he lived in La Cueva, a cave near Dripping Springs. In 1869, the Hermit's usual signal fire failed to appear on Friday. A rescue group found the Hermit murdered with a knife in his back. An ascetic hermit to the end, he was wearing a penitential metal girdle full of spikes. (Courtesy of NMSULASP)

La Cueva. A man leans against the entrance to La Cueva in the Organ Mountains. Once home to El Hermitano, La Cueva sits near the entrance of Fillmore Canyon, and remains a popular picnic destination in the Organs today. (Courtesy of NMSULASP)

Paleozoic Trackways. Paleontologist Jerry MacDonald brushes dirt from tracks in the Robledo Mountains made by a dinosaur more than 200,000,000 years ago. In 1987, MacDonald discovered the world's largest collection of insect and vertebrate tracks, now imbedded in sheets of stone, dating back 280,000,000 years. The site could become the Mesilla Valley's first national monument. (Photo courtesy of Jerry MacDonald)

Heavy Lifting. Jerry Macdonald poses in the 1980s with one of the slabs of stone containing ancient trackways which he back packed out of the rugged Robeldo Mountains.
(Photo courtesy of Jerry MacDonald)

Nuestra Señora de la Candelaria Church. Built at the site where religious services have been held since the 1860s, the church at Doña Ana was rehabilitated in the late 1990s through a youth work project coordinated by Pat Taylor of Cornerstones Community Partnerships. The crew replaced over 17,000 adobe bricks to stabilize the building. (Photo by Jon Hunner)

The Plaza at Doña Ana. The newly constructed plaza with the church as an anchor on the north side helps to revitalize the town. El Camino Real passed on the other side of the church. (Photo by Jon Hunner)

3

The South Valley

Samantha Alaniz, Regina Burgess, and Jon Hunner

Riding through the Brush. An unidentified burro rider, protected from the thorny mesquite bushes by his thick leather chaps and coat, searches the desert for livestock. Note that the lassos are also wrapped to prevent the thorns from sticking in them. (Courtesy of NMSULASP)

Rio Grande Valley. Before bridges spanned the Rio Grande, ferries transported cars, wagons, and people from one side to the other. As a state-wide road system evolved in the late 1920s and 1930s, dams and bridges began to provide quicker means to cross the river. (Courtesy of NMSULASP)

Water is Life. In the arid Mesilla Valley, the Rio Grande provides life giving water for humans, animals and plants, fish for food, as well as a place to wash clothes. The water, even though muddy, also allowed for play, as the girl on the right is doing. (Courtesy of NMSULASP)

The River as Refuge. The Rio Grande marked the boundary between the United States and Mexico. To flee the violence of the Mexican Civil War that lasted over a decade beginning in 1910, many Mexicans crossed the river and sought refuge in the Mesilla Valley. (Courtesy of Mary and Rep. J. Paul Taylor)

Fort Fillmore. In 1861, Union forces abandoned Fort Fillmore (near where I-10 and I-25 now meet) when Confederates from Texas captured nearby Mesilla. Before the soldiers left the fort, they destroyed most of the supplies; however, they poured some of the medicinal whiskey from the hospital into their canteens. Retreating across the desert under the hot July sun with only whiskey to slake their thirst, the Union forces surrendered on the western slopes of the Organ Mountains. The remains of Fort Fillmore seen here were excavated in the 1960s. (Courtesy of NMSULASP)

Managing Water in the Desert. To make the Mesilla Valley bloom, workers dug laterals to create artificial streams throughout the valley. The water impounded by the Elephant Butte Dam (finished in 1916 near Truth or Consequences) provided abundant water for the farmers and ranchers down river who now could grow water thirsty crops like cotton and corn. (Courtesy of NMSULASP)

Mesilla Dam. Dams like this west of Mesilla were built to divert the water to laterals that then distributed it throughout the valley. Built around 1917, the Mesilla Dam also helped prevent flooding from a swollen Rio Grande due to spring run-offs and summer monsoons. (Courtesy of NMSULASP)

Cantaloupe Truck. By the 1920s with Elephant Butte Dam water, cantaloupes and other melons became profitable crops in the Mesilla Valley. In 1928, an acre yielded 234 crates of cantaloupes which cost 42.8 cents a crate to grow and harvest. (Courtesy of NMSULASP)

Fertilizer from Fort Bliss. To help fertilize the fields in the Mesilla Valley, horse manure from the cavalry stables at Fort Bliss was loaded onto railroad cars and sent north from El Paso. (Courtesy of NMSULASP)

Grapes. In the early twentieth century, grapes served as the symbol on the official seal of the city of Las Cruces. In addition to its delicious fruit, grapes also were made into wine and brandy. Today, vineyards in the Mesilla Valley produce a wide variety of wines. (Courtesy of NMSULASP)

A Family of Farmers. Farming in 1921 required both young and old to take to the fields. Spread out over this potato field, the Boyer family of the South Valley pulls weeds. The Boyers (along with other families around Vado) came to the valley looking for agricultural opportunities and to escape the racism prevalent against African-Americans in other parts of the country. (Courtesy of NMSULASP)

Compressing Cotton. Located at the end of Compress Road, the Las Cruces Compress took the bulky cotton and compressed it into dense bales. (Courtesy of NMSULASP)

Cotton Mill. After the Elephant Butte Dam insured abundant water throughout the growing season, cotton became an important crop in the Mesilla Valley. To separate the seeds from the fiber and then compress the cotton into bales for transport, the Las Cruces Compress near the railroad tracks processed tons of cotton. Notice the Model A cars in the background. (Courtesy of NMSULASP)

Drying Chile. Chile is the state vegetable and consumed by many New Mexicans. Here, green pods had been spread out on the ground to dry and then were collected in baskets. Both red and green chiles are from the same plant, only the red chile pods stay on the plant longer and turn red as they dry. In 2006, Doña Ana County harvested 3,000 acres of chile worth approximately $8,500,000 which equaled 22 % of the state's total chile production. (Courtesy of NMSULASP)

Fancy Chile Pepper. The three wooden frames allow the "Fancy Chili Pepper" brand of chile to be bagged and sent off for processing. In addition to chile being the official state vegetable, the official state question is "Red or Green?" Waitresses and waiters across the state ask this question when customers order certain chile dishes. (Courtesy of NMSULASP)

Chile on the Roof. Even today, drying red chiles on roofs is seen around the Mesilla Valley. The splash of red on metal roofs signals the end of summer, as does the smell of roasting chiles. (Courtesy of NMSULASP)

Stahmann Farms. In 1926, Deane Stahmann, Sr. (pictured here in 1961) and his father, W.J. Stahmann, cleared 2,900 acres of land south of Mesilla where they planted cotton. In 1932, they switched to pecans, which are the only mass-market nut native to the United States. (Courtesy of NMSULASP)

Transplanting Pecan Tree Trunks. These hardy pecan tree trunks can easily be transplanted. Seedlings are planted close together and then thinned out and transferred to other lots. Mature trees need about thirty feet distance from their nearest neighbors. (Courtesy of NMSULASP)

Geese at Stahmann Farms. Left over from cotton farming days, the Stahmanns used Chinese geese to weed and eat insects among the pecan groves. Today the Stahmann Farms with its 128,000 trees on 3,200 acres produces between eight and eleven million pounds of pecans annually. With operations in New Mexico and Australia, Stahmann Farms is the biggest pecan producer in the world. (Courtesy of NMSULASP)

Sorghum Press. Using a horse or mule driven press to squeeze the sugary liquid out of sorghum plants was a popular method to create molasses and sugar in the Mesilla Valley. Notice the farmer sitting in a hole so that the boom will pass over his head. (Courtesy of NMSULASP)

Leading a Bull by the Nose. Even though this massive bull easily dwarfs the ranch hand, the ring through his nose provides a sure way to control the beast. (Courtesy of NMSULASP)

Tortugas Elders. Manual Ortega, seated on the left, was 106 years old at the time of this photo. Seated next to him was Col. Eugene Van Patten, who assisted the people of Tortugas. Behind them, descendents of Manual (including a great-great-grandson) join in the posed photo. (Courtesy of NMSULASP)

Native Americans met at Tortugas Pueblo. During the reign of Mexican President Madero (1911-1913), Native Americans from Mexico visited with Native Americans at Tortugas Pueblo, just south of the State College. Although the people of Tortugas are not a federally recognized tribe, some of them trace their ancestry through Isleta del Sur in Texas to the Pueblo of Isleta south of Albuquerque. (Courtesy of NMSULASP)

Matachine Dances at Tortugas. On the plaza near the church at the Pueblo of Tortugas, Native Americans from Mexico perform a Matachine dance, which dates back to Spanish Colonial times. (Courtesy of NMSULASP)

Our Lady of Guadalupe Church at Tortugas. Built in 1914 by a group of Tortugas residents, their organization, Los Indigenes de Nuestra Senora de Guadalupe (The Indians of Our Lady of Guadalupe) still exists today. The fiesta of the Virgin of Guadalupe in December continues to be a time of reverence and dancing at the pueblo. Every year as part of the fiesta, a pilgrimage starts at the church and winds its way to the top of Tortugas Mountain, also known as "A Mountain." (Courtesy of NMSULASP)

Four on a Pony. In 1905, Nellie Bishop and siblings Ethel and Charles share a ride with youngster J.B. Thompson in the south valley. (Courtesy of NMSULASP)

Burt Residence. In 1912, the Mesilla Valley residents of the Burt, Bennett, Casad, and Lane families gather at the Burt home across the state border in Canutillo, Texas. (Courtesy of NMSULASP)

Family Reunion at the Bennett Farm (1930). On the far left, Fabian Garcia (who was adopted by the Casad family as a young boy) joins Gertrude Casad Bennett with her baby. Maud Casad Mandell in the middle with the striped blouse stands in front of her husband, Humboldt Mandell. Patriarch Humboldt Casad is on the far right. The Casad/Bennett/Mandell family farmed and ranched a part of the Brazito Land Grant in the south valley. (Courtesy of NMSULASP)

Berino Schoolhouse. During the Great Depression, children at the Berino Schoolhouse gathered on the playground. Some of these students were children of the farmers of the African-American community in Vado. (Courtesy of NMSULASP)

Brazito Camp. In response to the Mexican Civil War waging just across the border, the U.S. Army established military camps like this at Brazito south of Las Cruces. In December 1912, this soldier tries to keep dry and warm in a desert snowfall. (Courtesy of NMSULASP)

Wedding Day. Tomás Marquez and Consuelo Maya sit outside one of their father's adobe houses on their wedding day in 1937. Consuelo, born in 1908, moved with her family from Arizona to San Miguel in 1915. Tomás worked at Stahmann Farms where he trained and cared for sixty work horses as well as tended sheep and geese. (Courtesy of NMSULASP)

A New Dress. Consuelo fashions a new dress for a litter of puppies at her feet in 1949 outside her in-law's house in San Miguel. Tomás and Consuelo lived at one of the five workers' villages at Stahmann Farms where they raised their five children. (Courtesy of NMSULASP)

Baseball at San Miguel. In 1950, Avelardo Armendariz on the left, with Heriberto Armendariz and Abran Armendariz get ready to go to the game. Avelardo and Abran are brothers. (Courtesy of Abran Lujan Armendariz)

Cooking at a *Matanza*. In the 1970s, Juan Chip and Abran Armendariz stir a pot of red chile and pork at a matanza in San Miguel. Matanzas celebrate birthdays, anniversaries, quinceañeras, torna bodas (the day after a wedding), graduations, baptisms, confirmations, and other events. (Courtesy of Abran Lujan Armendariz)

San José Church. In La Mesa, the San José Church has administered to the faithful for almost a century. Today, with exterior stucco covering the adobe brick walls, it still looks much the same as it did in 1913. (Courtesy of NMSULASP)

4

New Mexico State University

Peter Dean, Terrence Faulkner,
Jonathan Jefferson, and Jeffrey Schnitzer

Las Cruces College. The New Mexico College of Agriculture and Mechanical Arts (which became New Mexico State University in 1960) started in this simple adobe structure located at Amador and Alameda Street. It rented for $25.00 per month. Hiram Hadley, the first president of State College (1888 -1894), came from Wilmington, Ohio to Las Cruces for his son's health. (Courtesy of NMSULASP)

Looking East at New Mexico College of Agriculture and Mechanical Arts. The original campus buildings for State College around 1900 from left to right were Science Hall, McFie Hall (Old Main), Hadley Hall, and Wilson Hall. None exist today. (Courtesy of NMSULASP)

Sentinel of the Past. McFie Hall was the original administrative building at State College. The cornerstone laying ceremony for McFie Hall was held in the summer of 1890, with the building ready for operation by February of 1891.Mcfie Hall was destroyed by fire in 1910. (Courtesy of NMSULASP)

Wilson Hall. As one of the first of renowned architect Henry C. Trost's buildings on campus, Wilson Hall was erected in 1909 and leveled after a destructive fire in 1937. The building was used for Agricultural Studies. Trost developed the master plan of the University's "horseshoe" design. Five of Trost's buildings still exist on the campus today, and the Trost style influences the design of new buildings. (Courtesy of NMSULASP)

Graduation Day (1913). A crowd gathers in front of the original Hadley Hall for graduation ceremonies. The building was named after the first president of State College, Hiram Hadley. The building was torn down in 1957 after the current Hadley Hall, erected in 1953 west of the old hall, replaced it. (Courtesy of NMSULASP)

The "Huns" are Coming. In 1896, State College's baseball team's self-proclaimed nickname was the "Huns." (Courtesy of NMSULASP)

An Aggie Beginning. 1893 marked the first season that State College fielded a football squad. Members of the first graduating class, Fabian Garcia, Ray Larkin, and Oscar Snow, were part of this Aggie football team. (Courtesy of NMSULASP)

Women's Basketball. In 1910, students at State College enjoyed the games of this women's basketball team. The "AC" on the uniforms referred to Agricultural College. (Courtesy of NMSULASP)

Aggie Football. The 1902 football squad sits atop the stoop of a campus building. (Courtesy of NMSULASP)

Food for the Soul. A YMCA bible study group takes a few moments from their meeting to pose with the Reverend Hunter "Preacher" Lewis of the St. James Episcopal Church (seen on the top of the steps in his clerical collar) in 1909. (Courtesy of IHSF)

Reunion of the Class of 1894. State College's first graduating class gathered for their 25th reunion. From left to right are former President Hiram Hadley, along with the class of '94 members Agnes Williams, Fabian Garcia, Oscar Snow, and Ray Larkin. One class member, Lem McGrath, had died. (Courtesy of NMSULASP)

Fabian Garcia, Agricultural Innovator. Fabian Garcia was appointed director of the Agricultural Experimental Station at State College in 1923. His innovative research into growing chile and other crops transformed desert agriculture. Garcia died in 1948. (Courtesy of NMSULASP)

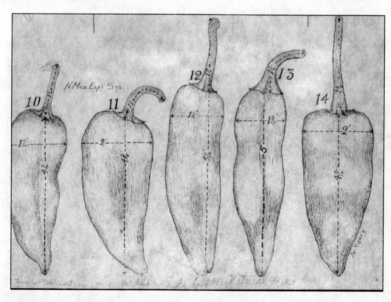

New Chiles from State College. Fabian Garcia revolutionized the study of the chiles of New Mexico through extensive studies and intricate sketches of the many different variations of the plant. His new breeds created less fiery chiles and helped make salsa the leading condiment in the United States today. (Courtesy of NMSULASP)

Miller Field Gates. These gates to Miller Field were built by the senior class of 1924. The athletic field, stretching north and west from the gates, was said to be the best in the territory. The gates were named for John Oliver Miller, who was registrar and volunteer coach of the highly successful football team from 1901-1908. In the background, Goddard Hall, named after the late dean of engineering, Ralph W. Goddard, was built in 1913 and is on the National Register of Historic Places. (Courtesy of NMSULASP)

Vista of Mesilla Valley. A view looking west from the bell tower of Goddard Hall in the late 1920s shows the agricultural fields central to the College's land grant mission. (Courtesy of NMSULASP)

KOB Radio Station. This radio shack, located behind Goddard Hall, was the first home of radio station 5XD, 5FY and KOB. It was the state's first radio station, created by Goddard after World War I. KOB was eventually sold to NBC and moved to Albuquerque where it became the "Voice of the Great Southwest."(Courtesy of NMSULASP)

Trans-Atlantic Test. A test which broadcasted radio signals to Europe took place from State College on December 12, 1922. The equipment in the radio shack was considered state of the art at the time. (Courtesy of NMSULASP)

Pioneer of Radio Engineering. Ralph W. Goddard (right) stands with Holly Lisle outside the KOB radio transmitter shack. Goddard started at State College in 1914, and became Dean of Engineering in 1920. During World War I, he trained enlisted men to send and receive wireless messages. Tragically, Goddard died from electrocution on December 31, 1929 inside the KOB radio transmitter shack. The University's current TV and radio station call letters—KRWG—were selected in his honor. (Courtesy NMSULASP)

Telephone Broadcast. KOB's Robert Stewart calls in the play by play of a New Mexico College of Agriculture & Mechanic Arts football game at Miller Field, ca. 1925. (Courtesy of NMSULASP)

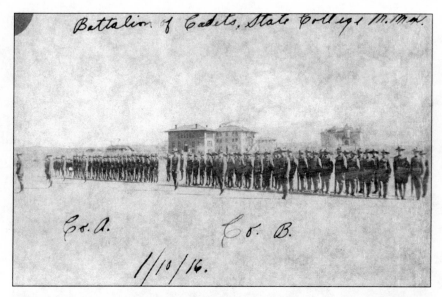

Attent Hut! Companies A, B, and C of the State College cadets stand at attention on January 10, 1916. The next couple of years would see some of these cadets chase Pancho Villa through northern Mexico and fight in World War I in France. (Courtesy of NMSULASP)

The Boys of Company C. Cadets from State College's R.O.T.C. program rested at Camp Pershing near the Organ Mountains in the early 1920s. Mandated by the land grant legislation that created the college, all able-bodied freshmen and sophomore men were required to participate in R.O.T.C. (Courtesy of NMSULASP)

Eyes over Las Cruces. This aerial view of State College in 1939 was taken from the southwest corner of campus looking northeast. (Courtesy of NMSULASP)

An Inspiration to All. Clara Belle Williams enrolled at State College in the fall of 1928. She graduated with a bachelor's degree in English in 1937 at the age of 51, and was the University's first African-American graduate. Ms. Williams also received an Honorary Doctorate of Law degree from NMSU in 1980. Clara Belle Williams Day, which renamed NMSU's English Building the Clara Belle Williams Hall, was held on Sunday February 13, 2005. (Courtesy of NMSULASP)

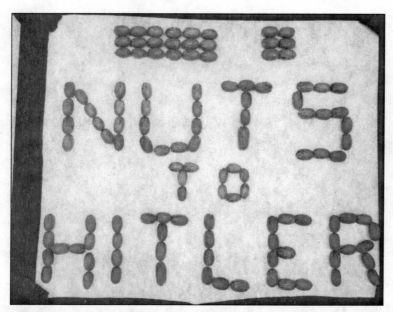

Nuts to Hitler. Fighting World War II on the Home Front, the Agriculture Department at State College advertised their opinion about the German leader. (Courtesy of NMSULASP)

Veggie Power. Land grant colleges across the country helped increase food production and encouraged responsible consumption during World War II. State College targeted both farmers and families with its "Vegetables for Victory." (Courtesy of NMSULASP)

Home Front. State College geared up for World War II, which included pilot training and aircraft mechanics. Students of the Smith Hughes course on aircraft mechanics break for a few moments to have their picture taken with the aircraft they built. (Courtesy of NMSULASP)

Gerald Thomas in the Cockpit. Gerald Thomas (President of NMSU from 1970 to 1984) was a strong advocate of the War Bond drive during World War II. The future President Thomas was photographed as a World War II pilot to help sell War Bonds in New Mexico and especially in the Las Cruces area. (Courtesy of NMSULASP)

Aggies in the Pacific Theater. Aggies fought in both Europe and the Pacific (and suffered in the Bataan Death March) during World War II. Pictured here in the Pacific from left to right are Capt. James Baird, Capt. Otis Horton, Col. Hugh M. Milton II, Lt. John Campbell, Capt. Mansil Schrivner, and Capt. Mark Radoslovitch. More than 2,000 ex-Aggies served in the armed forces during World War II, and 124 were killed in action. (Courtesy of NMSULASP)

The Era of the Veteran. After years of declining enrollment due to the war, the GI bill expanded enrollment so much that mobile homes were installed on campus to accommodate the post war boom of World War II veterans and their families. (Courtesy of NMSULASP)

Finding Time to Relax. Until Corbett Center was built, Milton Hall served as the student union where students bought textbooks, ate at the Cafeteria, or headed down to the basement to play billiards or bowl. Milton Hall was named after Colonel Hugh Milton. (Courtesy of NMSULASP)

Memorial Tower. The Tower was built in 1950 as part of the football stadium to commemorate the Aggies who had died in their country's defense. With the football stadium now south of the Pan-Am Center, the tower serves as the centerpiece for the College of Health and Social Services. (Courtesy of NMSULASP)

A Scene from College Road. Running east and west, College Road still exists but is now known as College Drive. Notice the bell tower of Goddard Hall to the right in the background. (Courtesy of NMSULASP)

Compassion and Service. Era Rentfrow, long time College registrar (1922-1962), was so determined to see students succeed that she personally loaned money to help students cover tuition, books, and board. After her death in 1988, the Era Rentfrow Endowment Fund carried on her tradition to benefit the student loan fund. (Courtesy of NMSULASP)

Making a Splash. The annual tradition of whitewashing the "A" on Tortugas Mountain, east of campus, started in 1921. Seniors at the base of the mountain mixed the limestone and water and then the freshmen (donning their traditional freshman beanies) and sophomores hauled the paint up the mountain to the juniors who splashed it on the A. Today, the campus Greek community keeps this tradition alive. (Courtesy of NMSULASP)

The Discoverer of Pluto. Although recently removed as a planet, Pluto was discovered by Clyde Tombaugh in 1930 at the Lowell Observatory in Flagstaff, Arizona. Clyde Tombaugh then came to State College in 1955 to teach in the Astronomy Department until his retirement in 1973. (Courtesy of NMSULASP)

Mock Funeral. NMSU students carrying a flag draped coffin protested the Vietnam War by staging a mock funeral. Milton Hall is in the background. Notice the black armbands on some of the students. (Courtesy of NMSULASP)

All You Need Is Love. Students protested the U.S. involvement in Vietnam in the early 1970s. Although NMSU avoided the violent anti-war riots that rocked other campuses, students did protest the war as well as the university's discriminatory practices and the policy restricting visits to dormitory rooms by members of the opposite sex. (Courtesy of NMSULASP)

8 Seconds is a Lifetime! A Rodeo Team member rides a bronco at the rodeo grounds east of campus. Rodeo was an important staple of college life in the 1960s and remains vital today, with NMSU's teams placing well in national competitions. (Courtesy of NMSULASP)

University Air Park. On the east side of the campus, the airport first opened its doors during World War II. The Aggies' Air Park was officially closed on September 30, 1971, partially due to the new Memorial Hospital situated close to the east end of the runway. (Courtesy of NMSULASP)

The Entertainment Hub of Southern New Mexico. The Pan American Center, constructed in 1968, has welcomed Bob Hope, Janet Jackson, George Strait, Elton John, and many others through the years. The Pan Am Center is also home court to Aggie basketball and volleyball and hosts the spring and fall commencement ceremonies. (Photo taken by Jeff Schnitzer)

Thanks for the Memories. Comedian Bob Hope is welcomed to NMSU by then President Gerald Thomas. Bob Hope came to Las Cruces in 1973 for a show to thank the Vietnam Veterans for their service. (Courtesy of IHSF)

Stadium Dedication. Aggie Memorial Stadium was dedicated on September 16, 1978. Present at the dedication were from left to right, Jim Masse, Howard Klein, Senator Lamar Gwaltney, Keith Colson, Mary Kay Papen, President Gerald Thomas (at the podium), Father John Anderson, Governor Jerry Apodaca, Rudy Apodaca, and Avelino Gutierrez. (Courtesy of NMSULASP)

An Aggie Welcome. The "Pride of New Mexico" Band welcomes the Aggie football team onto the field for the first time at the Aggie Memorial Stadium on September 16, 1978. (Courtesy of NMSULASP)

Skeen Hall. The newest building of the College of Agriculture and Home Economics was named after Joe Skeen, the long serving Congressman for southern New Mexico. Skeen Hall follows the architecture style of the university's first architect—Henry C. Trost. (Photo by Jeff Schnitzer)

Miller Field Gates Today. Seen here are the Miller Field Gates eighty-three years later than the photo at the beginning of the chapter. A plaque commemorating Miller Field Gates was unveiled during Homecoming festivities in 1999. (Photo taken by Jeff Schnitzer)

Memorial Stadium. At halftime of the inaugural home football game in 1978, the NMSU Marching Band puts on a spectacle for the hometown fans. This Memorial Stadium replaced the old one that was south of Williams Hall, the former gymnasium and the current Art Department. Both stadiums were built to honor the students of the university who lost their lives fighting in foreign wars. (Courtesy of NMSULASP)

Bibliography

Beckett, Patrick A. *Las Cruces, New Mexico 1881, As Seen Through Her Newspapers*. Las Cruces, N.M.: COAS N.M. Publishing and Research, 2003.

Chavez, Thomas E. *New Mexico, Past and Future*. Albuquerque, N.M.: University of New Mexico Press, 2006.

Foscue, Edwin J. "The Mesilla Valley of New Mexico: A Study in Aridity and Irrigation," in *Economic Geography*. Vol. 7, No.1. (Jan. 1931), pp. 1-27.

Griggs, George. *History of the Mesilla Valley, or, the Gadsden Purchase: Known in Mexico as the Treaty of Mesilla*. Las Cruces, N. M.: Bronson Printing Co., 1930.

Harris, Linda G., et al. *Las Cruces: City of the Crosses*, Exhibit Text for Branigan Cultural Center, 2007.

Hunner, Jon, Brian Kord, Cassandra Lachica, and Renee Spence. *Las Cruces: The City of Crosses*. Charleston, S.C.: Arcadia, 2003.

Las Cruces (N.M.) 150th Celebration Committee. *Passport to History: 150 years, Las Cruces 1849-1999*. Las Cruces N.M.: 150th Celebration Committee, 1999.

Las Cruces Bulletin

Las Cruces Sun News

New Mexico State University. *Mesilla Valley: The Rio Runs Through It,* www.cahe.nmsu.edu/pubs/resourcesmag/hotstuff/spring99.html.

Nuestra Senora de Candelaria, Doña Ana www.cstones.org/projects/ Archives/Dona Ana

Owen, Gordon, *Las Cruces New Mexico 1849-1999 Multicultural Crossroads.* Las Cruces, N.M.: Red Sky Publishing Inc: 1999.

Price, Paxton P. *Mesilla Valley Pioneers, 1823-1912.* Las Cruces, N.M.: Yucca Tree Press, 1995.

State of New Mexico. *Dripping Springs Natural Area, Watchable Wildlife Area Site No. 54.* www.wildlife.state.nm.us/publications/documents/ dripping springs natural area.doc

Taylor, Mary D. *A Place as Wild as the West Ever Was: Mesilla, New Mexico 1848-1872.* Las Cruces, N.M.: New Mexico State University, 2004.

Thrapp, Dan L. *The Encyclopedia of Frontier Biographies, Volume I.* Spokane, WA.: University of Nebraska Press, 1988.

Trumbo, Theron M., et al. *A History of Las Cruces and the Mesilla Valley.* Las Cruces, N.M.: Historical Data Committee of the Centennial, 1949.

Photos Contributed By: Dr. Abran Lujan Armendariz, Dr. Jon Hunner, Institute for Historical Survey Foundation, Rio Grande Historical Collection, Jerry MacDonald, the Taylor Photo Collection, and Jeffrey Schnitzer.